CW00571068

BOLD

A collection of curated poetry and prose
designed to document the myriad
images of masculinity.

BOLD

Brought to you by The Broken Spine

Art and Literature

ISBN: 9798386777357

© Alan Parry, 2023. All rights reserved.
001

Book design: Alan Parry and Andrew James Lloyd
Cover Art: Elizabeth Kemball
Eds.: Alan Parry, David Hanlon, Matthew M. C. Smith, and Katie Jenkins
All rights to individual texts are held and reserved by their individual authors.

The Broken Spine Ltd.
Southport / England / United Kingdom
www.thebrokenspine.co.uk

"masculinity is both *illusion* and *reality*"

JH Pleck

Dear readers and contributors,

Let me take this opportunity to thank you for making this purchase and/or sharing your work with us.

It's true that *BOLD* has taken a long time to come to fruition. It started as the spark of an idea in February of 2021 and by the end of that year we had opened for submissions. Then the wheels fell off. We lost funding and the project stalled. I brought in new readers and editors along the way and together we finally found the momentum to bring this anthology of masculinity themed creative writing to its completion.

I owe an enormous thanks to Katie Jenkins who joined the editorial team alongside David Hanlon, and it was us three who read what we believed would become the final document. However, it was not until Matthew M. C. Smith came on board that we were fully assembled. Some further snap submission windows followed to enhance the original manuscript. The writing that follows aims to document experiences and images of masculinity from several perspectives.

BOLD was initially inspired by my love for LadLit, Nick Hornby, Andrew McMillan, and by my own academic research.

Today, given the abundance of raging masculinity debates, the timing could not have been better for publication.

I'm delighted that I found that strength during some trying times to keep going, that you have decided to read, and that we have succeeded in giving your work the home it deserves.

Best.

Alan Parry
Editor-in-Chief

Contents

Put That Record On
Paul Robert Mullen

'Put that record on,' she said, falling through my bedroom door.

'Which one?'

'The one I really like.'

Balanced over the edge of the bed, I reached for the CD and flipped it into the player. She crashed onto the stacked cushions, almost spilling her gin.

'You should stop drinking so much.'

'Bollocks,' she scowled.

The record came on. A cotton shawl hung over bony shoulders. She wore a bright blue bob, black lipstick, orange eyeshadow and a tiny pair of denim shorts. Her tights were laddered from the calf up. She smelt like coconut and mandarin and alcohol.

'Love the socks,' she chuckled.

I looked down. I hadn't even realised. Christmas socks in February.

Take me out tonight…take me anywhere, I don't care, I don't care, I don't care…

She splashed her drink down perilously close to my brand new copy of *Ulysses* and pulled me up by the wrists.

'Dance with me.'

'It's not really dance music,' I said, sidestepping awkwardly.

'Dance with me!'

She leant over and switched off the lamp. We were silhouettes in a terraced bay window swaying to The Smiths in the moonlight. She gasped with pleasure, eyes closed, leaning back against the weight of my shoulder. Her acrid exhalations invaded my nostrils, and I noticed how frail she seemed for a twenty-year old.

The record finished and she fell back on the bed. I heard the front door slam.

'I'm home!' Kevin, my flatmate, shouted, poking his head in my bedroom door. He looked down at Cassie and shook his head.

'How was it?' I asked. He'd just done his final exam of the semester.

'Rough,' he sighed.

The headlights of an HGV swept across the street and the sound of someone laughing fell through the window, slightly ajar.

'Put that record on again,' Cassie slurred. Kevin rolled his finger round his temple. *Nuts*.

I put it on anyway.

...and in a darkened underpass I thought oh God my chance has come at last...

She rolled over, curled foetal, onto my pillows. By the end of the song she was asleep, her chest rising slightly, her shorts wedged high on her thighs revealing every groove and bow. I'd be sleeping on the sofa again.

I walked into the kitchen where Kevin was pouring two tequilas. He looked at me and laughed.

'You never learn,' he said, handing me the drink.

I'm Proud of All the Dreams I Never Had
Dave Garbutt

All of them and all the roles
I haven't played–
vengeful ghost, tall saturnine wizard
a street fighting man
a wolf in New York
the bright star, eyes squinted
at the sun a poncho over my gun
or sliding whiskey along the bar
to toast the absent me
for my children living by the railway station
of off to the park with nanny for a day
flying kites.

So I have been away
while you were growing
but it gave us a life,
food, memories, and tracks
up the hill, out of breath
dragging our sleds, like Scott,
and we stopped
on a round treeless top
to breathe
we looked around
snowy peaks and skies
mare's tails, the föhn,
and I opencd my hand
unclenched my fist
let you go   to ride
          first. By yourself.
I'm proud of that.

Surface Tension
Glenn Barker

Your words and hob-nail bile
ran over my touch-soft water, and
sharpened them into steel knife-edges.
Cut - sliced - diced, packaged
and stored, deep-coalesced.

Frozen they lie, deep-wedged ice,
layer on layer, hard, over a Baikal depth.
Skates groove and graze and scrape,
yet make no impression on my layers;
brittle-cast footprints, numb-cold to touch.

Show me a man, a mile high,
who doesn't pull his own blades
into the morning, past the heave and
sweat of inner quarried hours.

He's still searching for himself,
his flesh, his divided essence, surviving
on stucco chat; hard-trimmed, square-on;
hurt and honesty and touchstones repulsed.

The code of conduct remains intact;
stone silence, stone weight,
killing the air, anima and animus,
stone voices and gym-stares;
another round of steroid push and puff,
and snap-echo man-chaff: "I'm fine."

Lunch with Friends
Ronnie Smith

At far table's end seeking
the peace of anonymity,
her blue pearl eyes glazed.
The voice of trauma vibrating
just below her surface.

Across half-empty plates,
rolling his eyes to the ceiling,
laughing, hands narrating,
interrupting and contradicting.
In full voice, at the Earth's core.

She sees the finger wagging
across her own table, hears
the words in the doorway
of her kitchen, "Now just listen.
I'm speaking, see! Wrong again."

When His Voice Carries
Kate Dowling

Nothing else is
You wait for the sound
In your space
Anticipating his bell to chime the quarters
His words impatient until
The hours are rung out and
The minutes are wrung out and out and out,
Then stop.

A Letter to Copy
Devon Marsh

Low contrast of graphite on faded yellow
paper. I find his letter difficult to copy.

Dearest–he began, the word
appended to the left of her name.

I feel it proper to let you know
some of my final wishes.

I should like for Doctor Wilson to officiate.
For pallbearers I should like to have

two from our church… two from the lodge…
two from Capital Automobile.

With a sharp pencil on a legal pad
in two full pages he made no mistakes.

He apologised for the burden he'd become
knowing he would never work again

unaware his employer
would never stop his pay.

His present mind and his one good hand
conveyed his thoughts in flowing script.

His pencil had no eraser–

Damaged

Helen Laycock
(First published in *Frame*)

Papa chose his peach
with care;
ran his thumb
over the pile of its cheek,
cupped its weight,
bounced it like a baby,
caged it in his strong fingers
and teased its give,
then he would
break its flesh,
and as its crumpled
guts spilled
sweet damage,
it cried sticky tears.

They Look Up
Dan Duggan

Our children's irises catch the stars
because they are always looking
for our faces
for the reassurance
that moonlight brings.
To them, we are crowned
by the night sky, our hair strewn
with comet tails.
We are their twinkly-eyed gods,
our mouths full of magic,
the firmament draped over us,
like a meteor shower cap.
They succumb, spellbound
as we pour words through their souls
hoping that our kindness will catch
as their characters bloom
inside the orbit pull of our love.

What My Father (Not A Poet) Might Say

Italo Ferrante

(after Mary Jean Chan)

that he got pushed into his dad's open casket when he was 8
that I should get a mastiff and name him Nero
that watching two men kiss on TV is like watching chimps scratch
their bums and take a whiff
that he has never lost a tennis match in 56 years
that he will never accept blood from me
that watching two men kiss on TV is like watching a headmaster
staple the tongue of his secretary
that he would never shake hands with a man who shaves his groin
that he was tickle tortured by his uncle for playing truant
that watching two men kiss on TV is like watching a nurse fit a
catheter to an old sex addict
that I look like a meatloaf in my mustard jumpsuit
that he didn't raise his boy to be a daisy chain smuggler
that watching two men kiss on TV is like watching toddlers swallow
a fistful of washing pods
that I don't need therapy when I can get a self-help book
that he will call in sick to my wedding
that watching two men kiss on TV is like watching an elephant rip
off the bonnet of a truck
that he'd rather sell his forehead skin than change his family name
that he learnt to cure his loneliness with a cup of vinegar

Self-Portrait For & Against
Italo Ferrante
(after Chen Chen - First published in *Lighthouse*)

For my vegan decaf latte. For the cinnamon in Lana Del Rey's teeth.
For vanilla love-
making. Against the lilt of a harpsichord. For the Procession of the
Hooded. For the foot fetishist
who asked Simon of Cyrene to take off his sandals. Against Mary
Magdalene who gave Jesus a full body
wax for free. Against the reverend who shamed my moobs on
Discord. Against the underwear pantheon
in TK Maxx. For my mum who called me anorexic when I refused
the third serving of cannelloni.
For my mum's mum who set parental control on our TV because of
Måneskin. Against the Danish word
for moonlight. For the grave accents. For the silent letters. For the
vanishing hyphens.
For all the French colleagues I upset by wearing a Union Jack
onesie. Against art history
teachers who fucked girls with braces & daddy issues. Against
wanting to be one of those girls.
For the sexual awakening I had on a school trip to the Sistine
Chapel. Against being 10.
Against being 10 & dreading Adam's apples. Against being 10 &
dreading Adam's apples & taking pics
of Ignudi with a Nintendo DSi. For the barbers pulling my hair back.
Against William Carlos Williams.
Against my dad who would hit my mum on the temples. Against the
man who taught me how to glass
my dad. For The Cure. For The Stone Roses. For The Smiths.
Against Morrisey. For my sister who raised me
to broody basslines & blurry Polaroids. For Francesca Woodman
even if I've always preferred Cindy Sherman.
For all the exes I have hexed. For the Blackpool poet who
hypnotised me during a one-to-one tutorial.
For all the straight men who treated me like a piece of furniture. For
the retired man who bubble-wrapped

my dick for fear of getting COVID or AIDS or both. For the family
friend who kept sliding into my DMs.
For the Grindr date who blackmailed me. For the nudes that reached
my students. Against my will. Always,
against my will.

Father's Day
Kyla Houbolt

I do not go to God
as a petitioner
but as a participant, one fractal
of that light,
a prism going home
to play in the sunfield
like animals lying on the earth
their bodies so happy, the way
the earth
embraces without holding
like a whale sounding from the
deeps
like lava flowing forth
then returning
so I can become large
become small
become you
my enemy
whom God loves
just as much as me

The Good Samaritan
Aubriana Niven

108 degrees of angry summer is lighting the ground ablaze. He walks the rocky gravel barefoot, yet it doesn't faze him. His feet don't hurt nearly as badly as they did on the day he walked for hours on end in Afghanistan to find his fellow soldier hanged, not by an enemy's rope, but from the soldier's own. The overzealous August sun whispers to him in an uncharacteristically calm tone. Be still. Almost instantaneously his legs turn to stone and he collapses on the beachside bench he calls home. His body is in the foetal position, facing the backrest of the bench.

A family dressed in matching floral pastels stare at him long enough for his body to turn cold despite the august heat. The mother, a woman with vibrant auburn hair and a toothy smile, hands her daughter a one dollar bill to give him. Remember the Good Samaritan. Jesus had a heart for the poor, so do we.

The eight-year-old girl tiptoes to him carefully. She's afraid of him, afraid of God. The man's hairy body is now rigid, a residue, like sea foam, surrounds his mouth in a layer of white crust. She lays the dollar in his left hand. It curls around a syringe, a bent spoon, and a crisp dollar bill, fresh from the Bank of America.

Man Strength
David Hanlon

I'd never
thought of myself as manly
until I started lifting weights recently.

Is that how it works -
an action
& then the thought follows?

Masculinity always eluded me -
an escaped convict,
me - the high-security prison;

constructed by a construct,
emaciated to a polarity,
defined by a quality
I wasn't meant to be.

My walls gesticulated too much,
weren't strong enough
to dampen my effeminate tones.

Now, people tell me that I'm not *camp*,
but whenever I hear my voice
I still worry
that I'm detectable.

Kiwi skin boys spat:

Batty boy

Queer

Gay boy
Did it make them feel stronger?
More manly?
Less human?

I know now
how that strength is
holding one's breath underwater
with no way to reach the surface.

I know now that real strength
is knowing our
hearts are flowers,
& loving
the bloom
& withering.

Men's Health
Katie Jenkins
(A found poem using only text from an issue of *Men's Health*
magazine)

Overhaul your life:
men's health is about proactivity / unabating positivity
there's never been a better time to take control
you only achieve by pushing your boundaries / keep it real
if you want to improve / pick your personal antidote
habit building not resolve / be greater than whoever you are
today make yourself accountable / refuse to take no for an answer
grin at the spectre of pain and fatigue / you don't have to fake
something if it's real / work hard and make good
on your talents / ambition faith and confidence / realise
your physical and mental potential / make no excuses
you're crispy round the edges.

Do the reps:
pain-cave warriors / get your steps in / reps till you're dying
build up shred down / your body is a dynamic organism
you'll have to push yourself harder than you might think
health and fitness are for life / don't skip legs day / squat
constantly / a spot of power lifting / you must finish all the work
the man-maker rocks your body / dial up the endurance
keep your form decent / get ready to start shredding
this one's going to take grit / brace your core / avoid hitting
failure / repeat until you finally get stuck / lengthen your stride
gas out / discipline / most people thought it was impossible
repeating repeating repeating / an endless homage
every man wants to be bigger than dad.

He embraces his greatness:
unapologetic about who he is / won't stop until he's carved
eight-pack abs / his size can make him a target / he fights
to gain the advantage / he continues to rely on certain
affirmations / he looks for lessons / he's far more than the sum
of his trauma / the ease he enjoys has been hard earned / quick
to smile fast to laugh a happy storyteller / thoughtful
both on and off the field / longer leaner and steelily lupine
he gambols on / his stomach doesn't hang over his belt
his workouts have turned into his therapy / he's often
pulled over / striking his gloved fists into mitts
his tattooed arms ripple / his shoulders stretch
his hoodie / he'll reward himself
with a salad.

Extract fact from fad:
the beautiful people are everywhere / a study
of Navy Seals found / long periods of work impede
focus and accuracy / high performers display greater
consistency / losing ruins everything / repetitive work
is the price of success / gravity is a fickle friend
the safety net's full of holes / hardy people plunge
into icy waters / your commute predicts your day
yeast thrives on moisture / happy things make you happy
there are no magic bullets for mental health
masculinity is power / evening wood is not really
a thing / there is no one way to lead / the body
curbs the sex drive in time of stress / sperm counts
have been plummeting for decades / testosterone
can be easily purchased online / the eccentric muscle
is underutilised / men's health problems
are ignored by the mainstream media
a reusable straw spares your teeth
you can never win everyone's love.

Take inventory:
athletically inclined but chubby / underfed
and agitated / seventeen years left on the mortgage
a triple shot americano / a three-column system
a morning squat session / a metabolic advantage
rolling news and financial reports / a cleansing
of the body and soul / swingers club membership / a set
of baby love handles / the sex drive of a week-old
banana / organic heirloom variety / elastomer guided
to create a realistic ride / a new kind of supplement
a tennis match against your best frenemy
the home office / the humble press up / the after-work
rush hour / the throes of middle age / a seductive allure
existential millennial angst / drip-feed ingredients
the testosterone levels of an 80-year-old man
torque effectiveness and lateral force / mind-body
traumas and weight gain / a crucible for transformation
monolithic, oppressive everything
every defeat hurts.

Don't quit:
collision is part of the sport / work has been
overwhelming lately / drown post-shift adrenaline
with Jameson and Guinness / move in tandem with your body
channelling your inner monk / in a rush to get your fix
dial down the intensity / commit to meaningful breaks
drill down and find your patterns / gain mastery / stick
to what you know / parity of esteem / spit out the lines
this is falling with style / you have to get on with it
protecting endurance and vitality / there are alternative
ways to think and feel / talk to someone
teach someone to play the drums / find a mentor
don't ask for whom the bell tolls / you can only control
what you can control / talk to a doctor / watch
your numbers / disarm people with a joke and smile
serve with gravlax / tell me
what depression feels like / push back
push back up explosively
return under control.

Nobody
Alan Parry

we're in his bedroom listening
to Robbie Williams'
Old Before I Die on repeat

i move to change the music & he snaps my
Motown Greatest Hits CD in half

there are holes in his walls & you can see inside

if he finds out that i don't care for him
or even like him & that i'm only
here because there is nowhere else
he will end me

we're playing *Championship Manager*
& he tells me his girlfriend's mother
caught them fucking one afternoon
after college & i lie about my girlfriend,
from sixth form, who i say i
fingered in the common room

he laughs in my face
& calls me queer & I take it because
if i don't

i will have nobody

Spark
Jay Raffrty
(For Aubriana)

Have you ever felt someone like this before? I don't mean
held their hand, or brushed up against them as you walk
to class together. I mean have you felt them in a room
with you, like an open flame or a candle throwing it's heart
across the dark? It's the opposite of something being just
a little bit off. Not a crooked picture frame, asymmetrical ceramic
tile or a pixel dead on a screen. No this is the opposite. This is
something sublimely right. It's like you can hear the air melt around
them, you feel them before you've clocked eyes on them. The
electrical spark before a lightning strike or some other sixth-sense
shiver.

People like that come along rarely. They possess what more
spiritual folk would call an aura. Gen-Z would say vibe. You can
feel them in a room, like their presence warms you, they give
off something. It burns your skin but only the side closest
to them, like dew drying at sunrise but only on an east facing lawn.
You blush on half your face. The hairs on your neck stand
on end only if they're behind you. A singular source of static.

I've felt it once or twice. People like that, people that give off
something akin to waves, but much more consistent.
Much more human. People like that come along rarely.
Something radiates from them, something you can't quite name,
but you know feels good to be around. What I'm asking,
I suppose, is can you feel them too, when they walk into your life?
Can you feel the people like you?

Listen to the Grasshopper
Damien Posterino

I tried to walk on water for you-
my feet made star shaped ripples
as I started to sink
but you spent the entire time
smirking and scrolling on your phone.
You didn't even raise your head
when I stopped my heart beating
to create some suspense like an orchestra;
My only attention was a grasshopper
on a single green blade
rubbing his legs together in anticipation,
but his love song was for another.
Ants communicate via pheromones-
you can eliminate their chemicals
by spraying soapy water on them;
Maybe I should scrub my skin
with this homemade solution
so any unsent signals are permanently erased.
The male mockingbird is a more prolific singer
as it yearns for attention,
mimicking the sound of anything.
Somebody look at me, he says.

Adult Autism
Anthony Owen

Before I was special
I was an angel in formaldehyde.
I was a minotaur with bulging bollocks.
I was Perseus versus Medusa trapping her in my shield.

Now I am special
I am a jar of pickles prickling the palate.
I am a Roman statue the Visigoths defaced
I am the Zinnias bursting out from its fractures.

Man Up
Anthony Owen

In the guillotine of stratus
nights head dropped bloody
and I thought of my friend hanging.

My boss said he's worried about me
how everyone else has seen it too
he sent me a .gif to remind me I'm only human.

My friend died in a rope's eye
she loved horses so an apt departure
her neck galloping in horsehair.

My boss told me it's been three weeks
that it's time to man up and hit target.
I told him I'm only human to his face.

Woodwork
Barney Ashton Bullock

Our bevels sanded silky, knotted-
kinkeries inclined into concave curves,
all such glitches expunged or veneered.

The vice like grip of tension held us
deadlocked in a dovetail joint,
in splintering suspension,

in a web of complex chiselling nerves,
bouncing and rebounding
within our abject clamped stasis

and every affirmation mouthed
pounced on as click-bait;
reading the varnished intent within,

as ever, too late, too late!
But, oh, the smooth artisan beauty
of a man and his mate

in symmetrical sympathy,
in mortise and tenon fixity
of mutual conjoinery:

we nudged, in jilty niggles,
past the choking blunt blades
of cack-handed hams

and held fast as our lives
planed against the grain,
our kisses in the sawdust.

Al
Mark Ward
(after Patrick Proctor)

He talks about his boys,
all loyal alphas, equals
obsessed with the deal,
The sale held aloft.

He lets his trousers fall,
peels off his clammy shirt,
alms at his feet, the ideal,
a psalm in underwear.

He leans against the wall, fully
aware how fatal his calves are,
how the light enlarges his crotch,
just how small he can make me.

The Duel
Mark Ward
(after Philip Core)

When we wrestle   we cease
      to be   separate

I touch you   intimately
      like when you   took me
dancing   we two-stepped
      out into   the night forgetting
safety   our   beauty haloed with
      moonlight   the beach
ours
                       you wrench
      me off   my feet
their eyes   changing   everything
      an audience   braying
your limbs   a new context
      the capacity   for joy
deadened   you're careful
      for what is   a wrestle
if not passion   stopped short

Terrible Monuments
Lee Potts

I cut and burn each year
but the kudzu still comes back.

A root, hard and silent
as a thigh bone, must still be at work
under the shed I built after clearing
the landscape left by the last owner.

Dad would know how to take the last
of its life from it, even hidden there.

But now, it's too late to ask
and all his gardens but one
are gone -- fading like dreams
once they were left alone.

He knew dry spells made a new tree
drive its tap root to seek deep.

He also knew it had to be watered in
the day it was planted by leaving
a hose to trickle onto bare dirt
for the hours left until it was dark.

He'll never know his abandoned orchards
are already becoming forests.

There Was a Man
Matthew M. C. Smith

Someone in the crowd at the funeral said – "Now there was a man!"

I place the green beret on his coffin. Polyphony of Tallis's *Spem in Alium*. Black suits, black ties, clean white shirts. Inflections of colour from dresses and painted faces. I take back the beret and place my hand down for the last time.

The varnished wooden container lowers. Passage to fire.

In the name of the Father.

I crouch on my hands and knees over the red, plastic box where we keep some of my father's belongings. The attic with his unfinished train-set is dusty and the plywood sheets with tacked-down tracking and scenery will eventually be dismantled. I don't have the heart to do it.

I pull out a still-shiny, paisley-patterned album from the last century with dozens of photos of him: a freeze-frame as he digs a veg patch in the back garden garbed in a maroon jumper, a wild thatch of blonde hair and a bushy, ginger moustache, boot on a fork; another of him holding our first dog, Jody, a cross-breed and 'free to a good home' when she was just a puppy; a polaroid snap of him asleep on our brown settee under the lampshade in the early '80s with a paper Christmas hat on, my eldest sister asleep across his lap. I leaf through – family trips to London with the five of us smiling under Big Ben and standing in formation at the railings of Buckingham Palace by an impassive guard. More snaps of us – on day-trips to the Cotswolds, at castles, the beach or at his beloved Roman sites, Bath and Caerleon. I smile back at his smile, the one where he's as pleased as punch holding his first grandson.

Father and son. Flat image versus looming face. Choked grief dries out my throat, tears on my hands and fingers.

The Marine photos from the late '60s and early '70s reveal a side of him I still do not recognise, nor fully understand. Black and white images of him with the rest of his troop undertaking gruelling exercises on Dartmoor; a 30 mile speed march through a bleak, monochrome wilderness, with charcoal and anthracite-black hills and a grey, forlorn sky on a now-creased card – a sharp contrast to the almost-pure whiteness of training in Norway, plunging into one of those ice holes that stopped your breathing, a crushing compression of the chest.

There are close-up photos of him as rakish as a whippet, cleaning a rifle, sporting a crew-cut and a chipped tooth. The shot of him seated on an open army truck sweeping into a middle-eastern town is particularly dramatic. He must be 19 or 20 there. On the back, the photos are marked *Krater, Aden, South Yemen '67* in jagged, faint handwriting. There are parade photos in his 45 Commando regalia and an assortment of guys, unknown to me, from his regiment, unified by their khaki clothing and slim, muscular physiques. My father had disdain for bodybuilders, men he perceived as vain, stating in no uncertain terms that none of them would make it through basic Marine training.

My father could walk on his hands and do clap press-ups years after his military career, where he had to climb ropes and do hundreds of press-ups a day. He was approached about applying for the SAS. In the box, there is a faded green belt for a 28-inch waist, with scratched chrome water containers; two green berets, with the badges still shiny, should be bagged up as the green felt has small holes; there's an empty artillery shell and shooting trophies from cadets. 20/20 vision. One image is loose at the bottom, covered in shooting blanks that roll away when I take a corner. My father lying in a sniper position surveying Krater Town, providing long-range cover for service personnel making their way about this town that was to be evacuated when the sun set on this British colony in 1967, insurgency and freedom-fighting temporarily combatted with stop and search, roadblocks, lethal missions about town and execution by firing squads. In Khormaksar cemetery, the broken bodies of the dead lay to waste ossifying six feet under baked dust.

I place the remnants of straw back into the innards of Clem the dog, my father's only remaining toy from childhood. I imagine him clutching it at night, the only son of ex-patriates, in a cotton-sheeted bed at the family homestead miles out of Freetown, Ghana, or at boarding school where he was despatched at the age of 6, to experience far too young, the harrowing pain of detachment from his parents and sisters. 'You cried every night at first, but got used to it', he once said.

There's a letter to his parents on blue paper in blotched ink asking for a birthday cake and a list of all the things the boys do at Elston Hall: shooting, climbing trees, hiding in the woods, the boys' choir. A facsimile of gentrified, middle-class English boyhood, where he learned to make planes out of balsa wood, had a tuck box and read *The Eagle*. He mentioned one of the masters who was kind to the boys, taking them to play cricket in the evenings. I can hear the sound of cork on willow and a breath in the trees and this little freckled, fair-headed boy, who switches from solitary self-possession to mixing in with the rest of the boys, so many of a certain class and type.

I hold his hand day and night in the hospice, there as he pulses. I stay on a fold-down bed. Ten days and nights.

I still feel his hand as dry as the grit between his fingers in his desert posting. I touch, once more, his cool temple, seeing impressions of the temperature-controlled ward; his jaw-bone under skin like silk paper.

I run, I train, chasing a spirit haring away over the mountain.

In the name of the Father. Amen.

If Our First God Is You, Father, Then Tonight

Scott Lilley

(this piece uses parts of Andrew McMillan's *Martyrdom as a Golden Shovel*)

we've made our second god the arcade boxing machine. I
am watching now, in this sticky-pennied church, we've started
worshipping in hard right hooks. Our soles clagged, we are walking
on WKD, on Jäger, Stella men in genital sweat, we are walking back
to worship, where to watch is to offer yourself to compete; where to
abstain is to submit; where to compete is also to submit; where you
strike the lowest score, you score the lowest. And, my god, father,

the arcade boxing machine is not really our god, father, just
metal and cushion and bragging rights. And to suggest a
punch punches-in our own faith, or the boxing machine a spark
of deity amongst tombstones of 10-pence pushers, in
one way, would be reading too deep. Besides, *it's your
turn*, and, not unlike this groan pulsing in your groin,
the machine incants *Eye of the Tiger* in 8-bit cover, again.

9pm
Ben McCurry

sitting on hot, lilted sand,
with ghosts of glory,
lovers getting everywhere
sand slipping through my fingers
like her hair through his

a car door slams
alone with the fleece of the night
a wash of waves comforts me

watching a slice of green glass, embedded in the sable
as it is pulled towards relief by little tides
it's never gonna make it

it's gonna make it
emerald sparkling under the navy

knowing nothing, feeling nothing
finally

the glass breaks through
and ventures west, toward America,

i wonder
when's it gonna be my turn?

A Scrap of Screaming Blue
Matt Gilbert

The dead bird is dead,
Daddy, look, come on,
– Oh God, it's not my fault,
or is it? – I wondered,
pursuing my son reluctantly
towards a garden corner
in a café on the Vienne,
river busy shrugging off
its stricken friend already
– cat killed most likely,
mostly head by then, unbeaked,
though with plumage enough left
to reveal that once it had been kingfisher
– or to compatriots, *un martin pecheur*,
a proper feathered French republican,
so, with pointless wine glass still in hand,
I followed his gaze, concerned finger
pointing at a tiny scrap of body,
do-something eyes turned back on me,
Dad saviour, if only I could blow life back
inside this broken creature, but I couldn't
begin to explain my failure to even try,
ruffled his hair instead, sending awkward
telepathic 'I'm sorry that it's dead' signals,
thinking I wish, I wish, I could do more,
I can't, before steering his small self away.

The Things They Keep: Conversations with Griff

Lesley James

It is the early afternoon and he is sober and happy to see me. He's asked me to give him a really close shave, and I agree. Better than cutting my mother's toenails. I am touched by this physical contact as we never touch. He sends me for his aftershave, an elderly bottle of Brut. Pink and gleaming, a bit nicked at the corners because I'm brutal, he seems pleased and feels his face. He smells of angelica.

I have more patience than usual with his tales. *In the War. In Canada.* For once I listen and we chat. He sailed to the States on the Queen Mary, inflating condoms and floating them off the decks like balloons in a wry bon voyage. He makes embarrassed mouth-twists at talking about condoms. He shows me where he's hidden money from my mother for the pub. Up inside the lining of his RAF tie.

Now I've got a story for you. It would make a really good TV series.' Dog Tags'. He chuckles as he shares it. He's been thinking about this for a long time.

*It's set in Canada. There are these two families, and they are at the lake, at a resort, there are lots of people in the sunshine. The women used to go in gangs to ogle (*he said oggle*) the RAF boys stationed nearby. The RAF pilots were like film stars in the war and the lake was where everyone went to relax. Anyway, one of the women says, look there he is, that one there. And the RAF boy hears it. They call him over and he's Welsh and they're Welsh too, people who Went Over To Canada and they are from nearly the same village. And one of the sisters shows a lot of interest in the boy and makes a bit of a fuss of him. They chat away, and she points to his dog tags. And he explains what they are and what they are for.*
Anyway, they all make him feel welcome and invite him to their homes on his leave days, make a big fuss of him, and he likes them. Especially the one sister. The men of the family are mostly away, running their business. They run a honey farm-
    - A what?

-because they were all farmers before the pit. Lots of fields and bees in Canada. The sister who likes the RAF pilot is married to the son of the other family. No children. And here we get to it. Her husband can't give her children. He'd had cancer, of the y'know, testicles, and when he survived, both the families upped-sticks to Canada for a better life. They put all their savings together and off they went. And then, to get back to the story, they put it to him. Would the RAF boy do them all a great favour? We want our grandson to be Welsh, they say.

There's a heck of a moment and he looks at me from under his eyebrows. He grins.

And then after the war the family goes back to visit relatives in Wales. They go to a pub and the landlord of the pub is there behind the bar and as he leans forward to collect some glasses, the dog tags come out from his shirt and clink against a pint glass and they see them, and - Dog Tags.

He chuckles, pleased with himself. I've enjoyed it too and wish there had been more.

Later that night, as I am shovelling him into my Mini, his metal crutch banging the paintwork, I am not so entertained. I've heaved him up from the tiles in the urinal of The Great Western, soaked in other people's pee, as pissed as pissed can be. He fights me every step out of the pub. People are looking. I sense they don't like me, they like him and I am the enemy, taking him home. I suppress my rage. He refuses to wear his seatbelt and in my head I play through the scenario of a crash.

Getting him up the stairs of the flat is the next test. He goes all floppy to resist as I shove him; he's laughing when I finally push him onto the landing carpet. He rolls like a woodlouse. I run back downstairs to collect his stick, or he'll never get up.

My mother's at the top of the stairs so the screeching and crying begin straight away. I pour myself a whisky and take the bottle to my room just in case he grabs it. He always wants more to drink once he gets to this point, and will do it to inflame her anger and defy her, assert himself, drink himself to death. My bedroom door does not close properly; my mother likes it that way, but I force it shut to dull the shouting.

The sounds of childhood, the same words in a different place, different time. *Bastard bitch.* That's a classic, unchanged favourite. I haven't heard *You're a whore and a prostitute* for some years, however. Aren't they both the same thing?

And here we are, sinking into that old normal, the feelings in their peculiar lukewarm cocktail: dread, annoyance – *Will you both be quiet!* - listening out for cracking of bones/calls for help. Tedium, unhappiness, sleep.

After he died, going through his things, I find a newspaper cutting. It crumbles like leafmould in my hand. There's a photograph of seated older folk, in a semicircle, backed by standing, younger men and straight-backed women, formal, shyly smiling. And the headline:

Three Generations Honour Their Parents
Canadian emigres return to Brynycwm

Then I find a photograph, sepia, smelling of camphor. One among hundreds of wartime shots in a suitcase, tumbled with empty albums, black pages ripped, denuded of all but the silver mounting corners.

A straight-backed woman is wearing my father's RAF uniform jacket, smiling shyly. There's a truck in the background: Watkins Honey. Her handwritten message to him, in sloping, blue-black script:

To Griff - Dad insisted this should be sent, so when
you have seen it please tear it up quick as you can

PLEASE

Goodbye
David Hay

Above monuments of ash,
Fermented leaves cascade down the sky
And eyes thick and buttery
View nameless landscapes
Made of shadowed dreams and blue-bottle wings
That create bridges in the sky,
Leading to regions unknown by vision or touch.

Magicians of the social shroud and strut,
Eyes smeared with futures comfortable and predictable
Whisper dark nothings to the heart of every star.

With my homeless stare,
And clothes styled on the dead,
I pick up a worm,
Raise it to the sun,
As if it symbolised all man's fragility
Before tulips drenched in the orange blood of the sun
Erupt out of his eyes,
Its stems burned into the smoke of sorrow.

I breathed in my last childhood dreams
And coughed until my throat slicked with fire
Birthed from the devil's first laugh
Spits out dust.
Eat the open wind I shout,
Madness kissing my eyelids
Until they're like sardines dripping with autumn sadness.

Gone! The pigeon cries,
Notes clicking against the stars,
Fastened on the lightning,
Slicing through thunder

Until its fruitless rage is held in my bowels
And expelled until I see myself an old man,
Unable to discern the toilet from the sink.
The hours cannot contain my grief,
I get up, go to work, smile and pretend
My brain isn't throwing up toxic fumes.

Oh lord, when did I become predictable,
Swifts pour down the black hole of the sky
Into my open mouth, becoming one with my blood
Cells within cells within cells.

Goodbye mum, goodbye forever.

Dancing on the Touchline
Stevie Harrison

Circus strong man plays out the magic
conjures the drama, slaps hands
groans grunts
grunts groans
makes a song and dance of it
leopard leotard straining every sinew.

Cannon-ball dumb-bells tremble
wait for three lights as talcum powder
floats as light as the dancer lifted by his partner
makes it look easy
makes a dance to a song about it.

A drop-kick from The Phoenix
oiled thighs dance down the touchline
side-step the tackler
waltz around the full-back
fist pumps the crowd
close enough to smell the liniment
cools down stretches like a dancer
pack of players seek the Headingley Hi-Life
enter Kiko's
watch the dancers
balance Tetley's on a radiator
leer the bodies in The Chiaroscuro
pick up the pint with wrecking ball fingers
stay on the touchline
until the last dance.

41

42

Printed in Great Britain
by Amazon

21084356R10032